MW00941245

Joy
To The
World

_____

GIVEN TO

_____

OCCASION

_____

DATE

Joy to the World
Copyright © 2004 by Tommy Nelson,
a division of Thomas Nelson, Inc.
All Rights Reserved

Artwork Copyright © 2004 by Precious Moments, Inc.
Licensee, Thomas Nelson, Inc.
All Rights Reserved

Bible text from the International Children's Bible.
Copyright © 1986, 1988, 1999 by Thomas Nelson, Inc.
All Rights Reserved

Printed in the U.S.A.
1 2 3 4 5 6 7 8 9 10 - 09 08 07 06 05 04

> ## "...I am bringing you some good news. It will be a joy to all the people...."
>
> ### Luke 2:10

Imagine that first, cold Christmas morning—the brightness of the nighttime stars now dimmed only by the dawn's rippling rays. It is quiet, except for the soft sound of cattle grazing nearby, and the gentle coo and occasional cry from a newborn baby. The King of all creation has come—and has come as a little child.

Though two thousand years removed from that moment, we still celebrate the joy of Jesus' birth at Christmas. This year, before the food and festivities begin, enjoy the calm quiet of the morning as your family comes close to the Christ child through the loveable *Precious Moments* characters from renowned artist Sam Butcher. *Joy to the World* paints poignant scenes from the Christmas story with select Scripture portions that capture the essence of Christmas in soft, pastel color. The new tradition will take you back to that special day so long ago, and keep your family close for every Christmas to come.

"For God loved
the world so much
that he gave his only Son.
God gave his Son so
that whoever believes
in him may not
be lost, but have
eternal life."

John 3:16

The angel came
to her and said,
"Greetings!
The Lord has
blessed you and
is with you."

Luke 1:28

"She will give birth to a son. You will name the son Jesus. Give him that name because he will save his people from their sins."

Matthew 1:21

The Word became
a man and lived
among us. We saw his
glory—the glory that
belongs to the only
Son of the Father.
The Word was full of
grace and truth.

John 1:14

"He will be great,
and people will call
him the Son of the
Most High. The Lord
God will give him the
throne of King David,
his ancestor."

Luke 1:32

The angel said to them,
"Don't be afraid,
because I am bringing
you some good news.
It will be a joy to all
the people. Today your
Savior was born in David's
town. He is Christ,
the Lord."

Luke 2:10–11

"This is how you will know him: You will find a baby wrapped in cloths and lying in a feeding box."
...So the shepherds went quickly and found Mary and Joseph. And the shepherds saw the baby lying in a feeding box."

Luke 2:12, 16, 17

"Give glory to
God in heaven,
and on earth let
there be peace to
the people who
please God."

Luke 2:14

Sing to the Lord
and praise his name.
Every day tell how
he saves us.
Tell the nations
of his glory.
Tell all peoples
the miracles he does.

Psalm 96:2-3

Shout to the Lord,
all the earth.
Serve the Lord
with joy.
Come before him
with singing.

Psalm 100:1–2

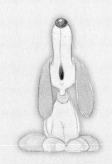

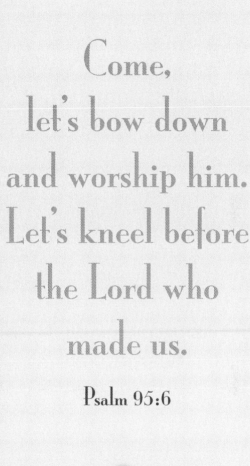

Come,
let's bow down
and worship him.
Let's kneel before
the Lord who
made us.

Psalm 95:6

Every good action
and every perfect gift is
from God. These good gifts
come down from the
Creator of the sun,
moon, and stars.
God does not change
like their shifting
shadows.

James 1:17

"...I taught you
to remember the
words of Jesus.
He said, 'It is more
blessed to give
than to receive.'"

Acts 20:35

This is the
day that the Lord
has made.
Let us rejoice
and be glad
today!

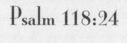

Psalm 118:24

We rejoice in him.
We trust his
holy name.
Lord, show your
love to us
as we put our
hope in you.

Psalm 33:21–22

"I leave you peace.
My peace I give you.
I do not give it to you
as the world does.
So don't let your
hearts be troubled.
Don't be afraid."

John 14:27

Praise the Lord
for the glory of
his name.
Bring your
offering to him.
Worship the Lord
because he is holy.

1 Chronicles 16:29

"The virgin will be pregnant. She will have a son, and they will name him Immanuel." This name means "God is with us."

Matthew 1:23

Depend on the Lord.
Trust him, and he will
take care of you.
Then your goodness
will shine like
the sun.

Psalm 37:5–6

Examine and see
how good the
Lord is.
Happy is the
person who trusts
the Lord.

Psalm 34:8

...And everyone is
friends with those
who give
gifts.

Proverbs 19:6

But Christ died for
us while we were
still sinners. In this
way God shows
his great love
for us.

Romans 5:8

"For God loved the world so much that he gave his only Son...."

John 3:16

Don't worry. We don't have to match His gift. We never could. God asks only one thing of us, as He extends to us the greatest gift of all: receive it—receive Him. And in that package wrapped up before time you'll find all the love, forgiveness, and acceptance you will ever need. In addition, you actually become a part of God's own family, reserving the right to revel in your prize—Jesus Christ—from now until eternity.

This year, as your family gathers around the tree to exchange their gifts and delight in each other's company, remember Him. Remember the Unseen Guest, His unseen Gift, and give back to Him the only gift you can—your heart.

PAINT